RACE IT!

Caroline Alliston

Quarto Library

Quarto is the authority on a wide range of topics.

Quarto educates, entertains and enriches the lives of our readers—enthusiasts and lovers of hands-on living.

www.quartoknows.com

Developed and written by: Caroline Alliston MA(Cantab), MSc, CEng FIMechE
Illustrator: Tom Connell
Photograper: Michael Wicks
Model maker: Fiona Hayes
Consultants: John Harvey BEng, CEng MIMechE,
Dr. Alex Alliston MA(Cantab), CEng MIMechE
Design and editorial: Starry Dog Books Ltd

This library edition published in 2019 by Quarto Library, an imprint of The Quarto Group.
6 Orchard Road, Suite 100
Lake Forest, CA 92630
T: +1 949 380 7510
F: +1 949 380 7575
www.QuartoKnows.com

ISBN 978-0-7112-4221-0

Manufactured in Dongguan, China TL012019

9 8 7 6 5 4 3 2 1

MIX
Paper from responsible sources
FSC® C104723

INTERNET SAFETY

Children should be supervised when using the internet, particularly when using an unfamiliar website for the first time. Publisher and author cannot be held responsible for the content of the websites referred to in this book.

CONTENTS

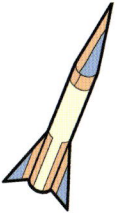

FOREWORD

Be inspired to make our world a better place.

We live in a "made" world. Without the advances made by engineers and scientists, we simply would not have the houses, cars, food, clothes, health care, and entertainment that we enjoy. Today we face truly global challenges, such as feeding a growing population and combating climate change.

This book provides five exciting and engaging projects to encourage creative thinking and problem solving. I hope it will inspire future generations of engineers and scientists that are needed to make our world a better place.

Dr. Colin Brown CEng FIMechE, FIMMM,
CEO, Institution of Mechanical Engineers

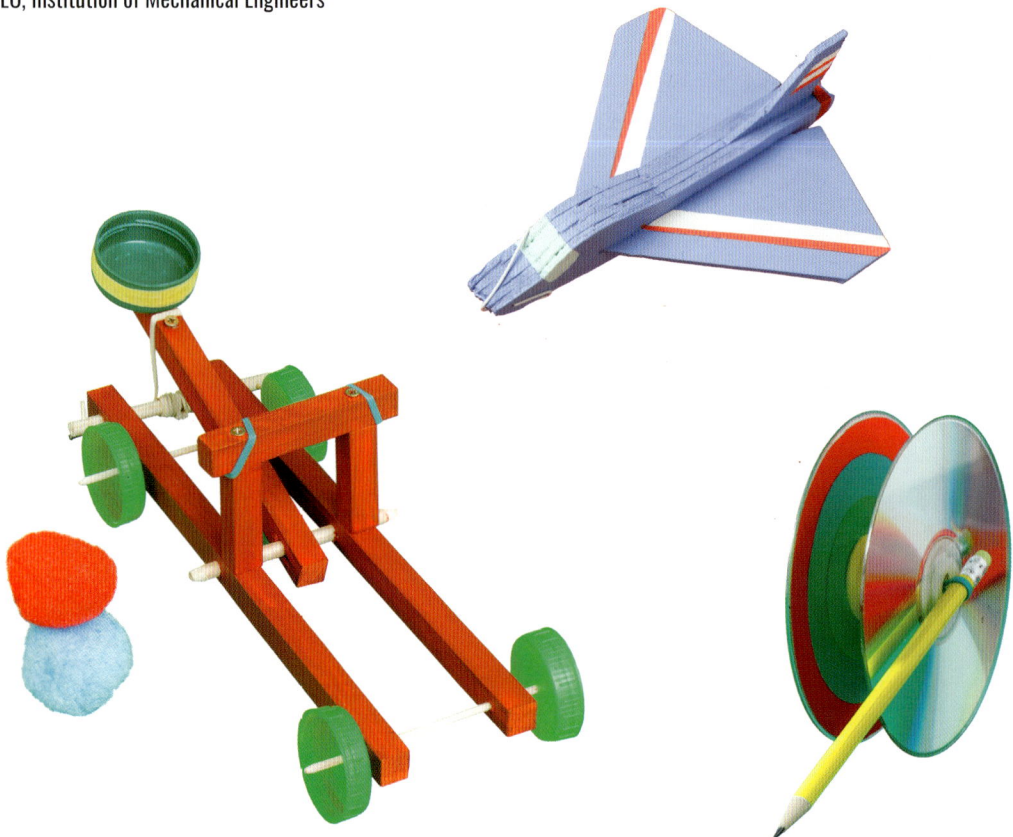

BE INSPIRED!

Test your design, creativity, and engineering skills with these five exciting projects and challenges.

WORK SAFELY

Always get permission from an adult before beginning a project and ask for their help when necessary.

SCISSORS
Be careful not to cut yourself with scissors. If using nail scissors, don't poke yourself—ask an adult to start the cut for you.

WOODEN SKEWERS
To avoid injuries, cut about 1/4 inch off the sharp tips, leaving the sticks slightly pointed to help you assemble the models.

GLUE GUNS
Only use low melt temperature glue guns; high melt glue guns can burn you badly. Use a gluing mat to protect your table. Avoid getting glue on your clothes. Make sure your hands and gluing area are dry before you switch on a glue gun. If you don't have a glue gun, most of the models can be made using double-sided foam tape—we recommend 1/2 inch wide x 1/32 inch thick, super-sticky.

USING ELECTRICITY
Always be careful when using electricity. Make sure you operate electrical appliances correctly and safely.

JUNIOR HACKSAWS AND DRILLS
Make sure you clamp your work in the vise so that you don't cut your fingers.

BRADAWLS AND SHARP PENCILS
Be careful not to poke yourself with bradawls and sharp pencils, and don't put them near your eyes.

GET READY

Before you start a project, make sure you have at hand all the tools and materials that you'll need—each project has its own YOU WILL NEED list. Then read the easy-to-follow, illustrated, step-by-step instructions to find out how to make the models. Discover more in the NOW YOU CAN activities and HOW IT WORKS explanations.

Cheap, everyday, and recycled household objects are used wherever possible. Collect old CDs and DVDs, thin sheets of polystyrene foam, plastic bottle caps, rubber bands, and plastic drink bottles.

Wood and fasteners can be bought from home improvement stores.

TAKE CARE!

Look out for the "Take Care!" symbol, which refers you to the warning instructions on the first page of each project. Craft knives, power tools, and small pruning shears should only be used by an adult.

1 thread spool

2 old CDs/DVDs

rubber bands (different sizes)
$1/32$ inch thick x about $1/8$ inch
wide x 3–3.5 inches long

1 eraser

1 M10 washer
plastic (preferably)
or metal

1 pencil

FROM YOUR TOOLBOX:

• sandpaper • low melt
glue gun or double-sided
foam tape • skewer or wire
paper clip

CD RACER

Wind up the rubber band and set your CD racer speeding across the floor.

1 Remove any paper labels from the ends of the thread spool. Stick a CD onto one end.

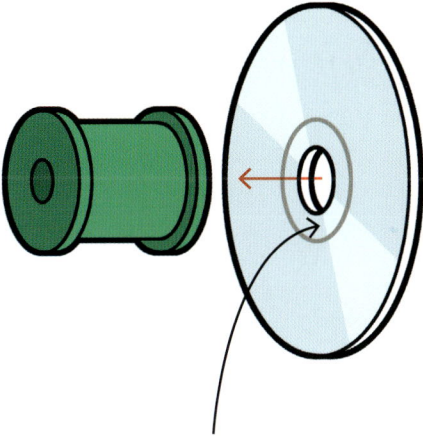

Roughening the surface of the CD slightly with sandpaper will help the glue to stick.

2 Stick the second CD onto the other end of the thread spool.

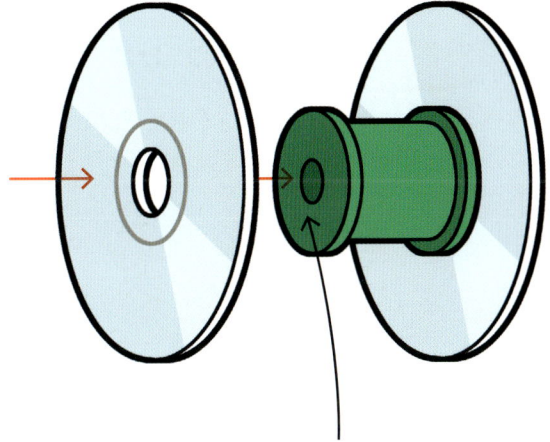

Make sure the holes in the middle line up and are not blocked with glue or tape.

3 Thread a rubber band through the central hole, leaving loops sticking out on either side.

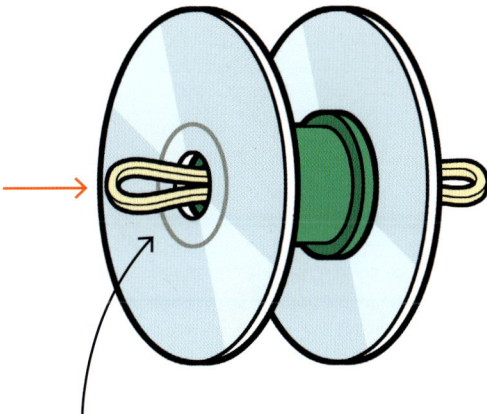

You can push the band through with a skewer or pull it with a hook made from a paper clip.

4 Push the eraser through one of the loops in the rubber band.

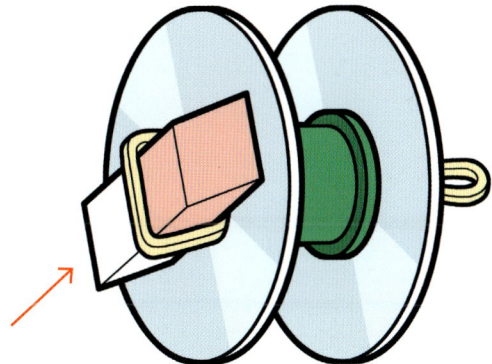

5 Push the other end of the rubber band through the washer, leaving a loop sticking out.

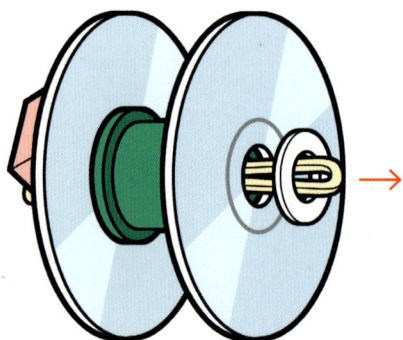

6 Push the pencil through the loop in the rubber band that's next to the washer.

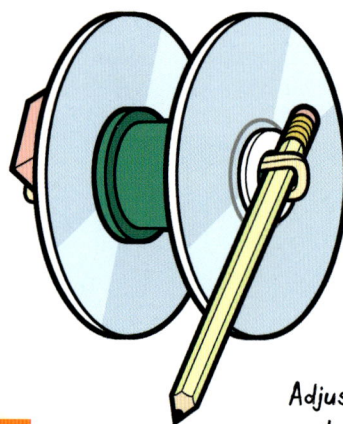

Adjust the pencil so that the pointed end sticks out much more than the other end.

TIPS & HINTS...

The rubber band should be just loose before you start winding it up with the pencil. If your rubber band is tight, swap it for a longer one, otherwise the extra friction will slow your racer down. If it is too loose, try a shorter band.

7 To wind up your CD racer, hold the eraser with one hand and use the other hand to turn the pencil around about ten to fifteen times. Feel the resistance increasing as you turn the pencil.

8 Place your CD racer on a smooth surface with the pencil pointing backward. Let go and watch the racer go speeding across the floor!

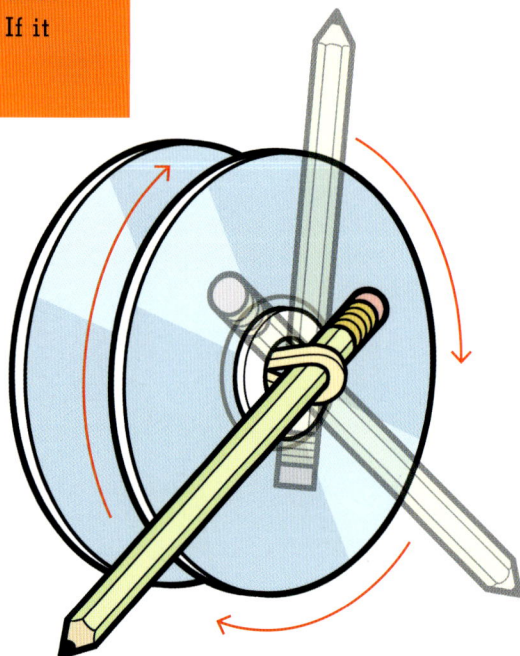

If you don't turn the pencil enough times, the CD racer won't go far. If you turn it too many times, the rubber band may snap.

HOW IT WORKS

The CD racer converts elastic potential energy in the wound-up rubber band into movement (kinetic) energy as the rubber band unwinds, making the racer move across the floor. Energy is also converted into heat and sound due to friction between the moving parts.

As the rubber band unwinds, it turns the eraser (made from a high friction material that grips well), and as the eraser turns, the CD unit turns with it. The washer has low friction, allowing the CD unit to turn while the pencil stays pointing the same way. The tip of the pencil has quite low friction, allowing it to slide easily across a smooth surface.

NOW YOU CAN...

★ Wind up the rubber band by different amounts and compare how far the racer travels.

★ Experiment with different lengths or widths of rubber band to try to improve your racer's performance.

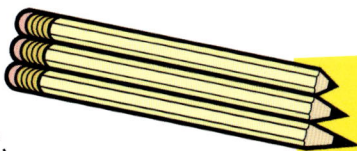

★ Sharpen the pencil or adjust it so that it sticks out more or less.

★ Change the washer material or lubricate it with dishwashing liquid or bicycle oil to reduce friction.

★ Test the CD racer on different surfaces.

★ Challenge a friend to a Formula One CD race!

TEDDY BEAR ZIP WIRE

Construct a zip wire and send your teddy bear whizzing across the room!

1 plastic pulley
about 1 ¼–2-inches diameter,
³/₁₆–¼ inch central hole

2 old CDs

2 plastic bottle caps

1 wooden skewer

1 teddy bear or similar toy,
weight 2–18 ounces

16 feet of string

FROM YOUR TOOLBOX:

• sandpaper • low melt glue
gun • marker • adhesive putty
• pencil sharpener • pencil
• large scissors • small
pruning shears • ruler

TAKE CARE with the sharp pencil. Only adults should use the small pruning shears.

1 Using sandpaper, roughen the surface of the CD inner circles. Glue the pulley to these surfaces, lining up the centers.

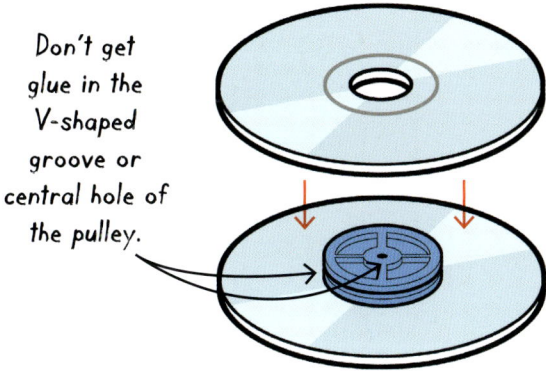

Don't get glue in the V-shaped groove or central hole of the pulley.

2 Look carefully at the bottle caps. Mark a spot on the outside of each one, between any ridges on the inside or outside, as shown.

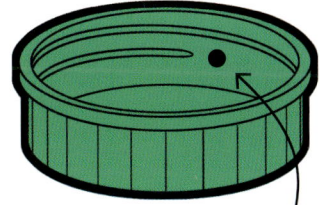

The mark is where you will pierce the cap.

3 Push the cap onto a lump of adhesive putty. Use a sharp pencil to pierce a hole in the side wall. Make a second hole in the top. Repeat with the second cap.

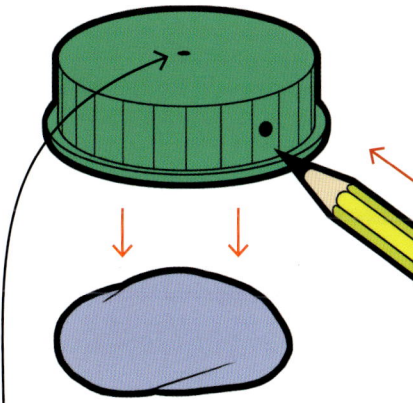

4 Use the scissors to cut off the sharp tip of a wooden skewer. Slightly sharpen the blunt end and slide it through the central hole in the pulley/CD unit.

Both ends should be slightly sharpened but not spiked.

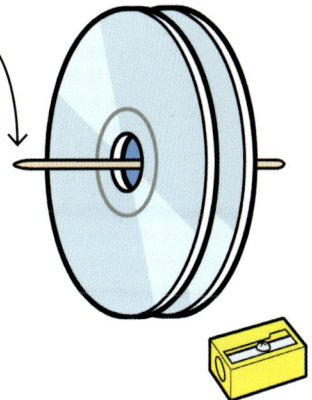

This hole will need to be a tight fit on the skewer.

5 Slide on the two caps, open ends outward. Hold the skewer and spin the CD unit to check that it rotates freely.

If the pulley doesn't rotate freely, try moving the caps apart slightly.

Leave a small gap.

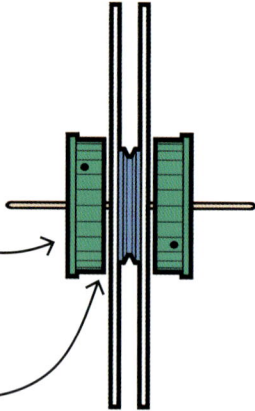

6 Rotate the caps so that the holes line up, as shown. Ask an adult to cut off the ends of the skewer with small pruning shears.

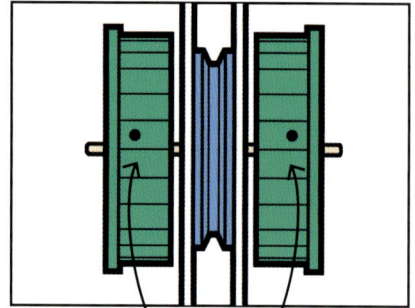

⚠️

Holes are lined up.

7 Cut two 16-inch lengths of string. Tie one end of each around your teddy bear's paws. Push the other ends through the holes in the caps, check that the strings are the same length, and knot the ends.

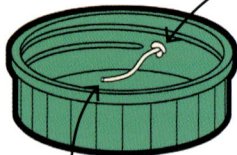

You may need to enlarge the hole with a pencil.

If the end of the string is frayed, trim and twist the cut end before pushing it through the hole.

8 Tie the remaining string to a door handle. Feed the other end under the pulley and hold the end tight. Lower it to make your teddy bear zip toward you and raise it to make teddy bear zip away.

HOW IT WORKS

The teddy bear travels down the sloping string due to gravity. If the CD/pulley unit with the teddy bear attached simply slid down the string, there would be high friction and this would make it hard for the pulley to move. However, because the CD/pulley unit is free to rotate, it rolls down the string. This reduces the friction, allowing the teddy bear to zip down even a shallow slope.

NOW YOU CAN...

* Experiment with the string at different slopes to see what effect this has.

* Try slackening the string a little so that the teddy bear slows down at the end of the ride instead of crashing.

* Push the bottle caps up against the CD/pulley unit to stop it rotating. How steep a slope do you need now for the teddy bear to move?

* Set up zip wires around your room or down the stairs—but warn your family first!

* Attach a string to your teddy bear so that you can pull it back up when it has finished its ride.

* Experiment using teddy bears of different weights to see which goes fastest.

1 photocopy (enlarged
170 percent) of
glider template

2 large polystyrene
foam discs $3/16$ inch thick x
12 inches or more
in diameter

Wire paper clips
various sizes

GLIDER

Make a polystyrene foam glider and
send it soaring across the room.

FROM YOUR TOOLBOX:

- large scissors • felt-tip pen
- nail scissors • tape
- paints (optional)

⚠ **TAKE CARE** Only adults should use the craft knife.

1 Take a photocopy of the glider template, enlarging it by 170 percent so that it fits onto one 11 x 17-inch sheet of paper or two sheets of printer paper.

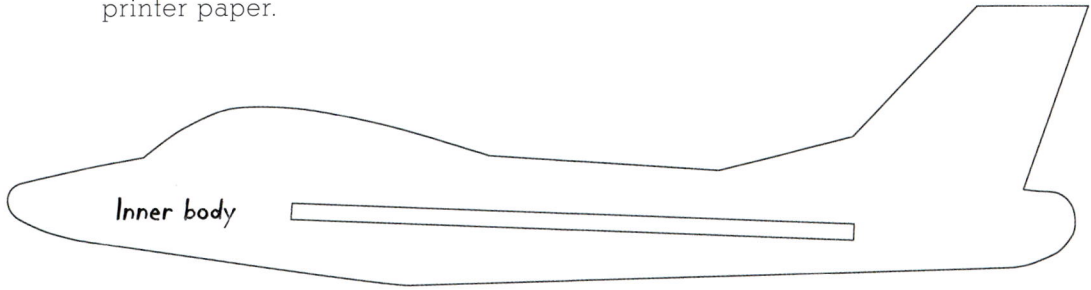

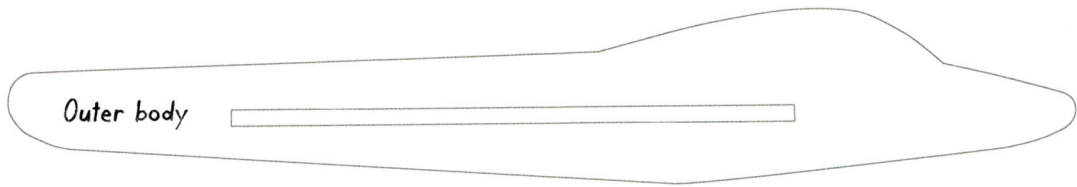

Inner body

← 10 inches →

Outer body

Use nail scissors to cut out the slots.

Use large scissors to cut out the pieces.

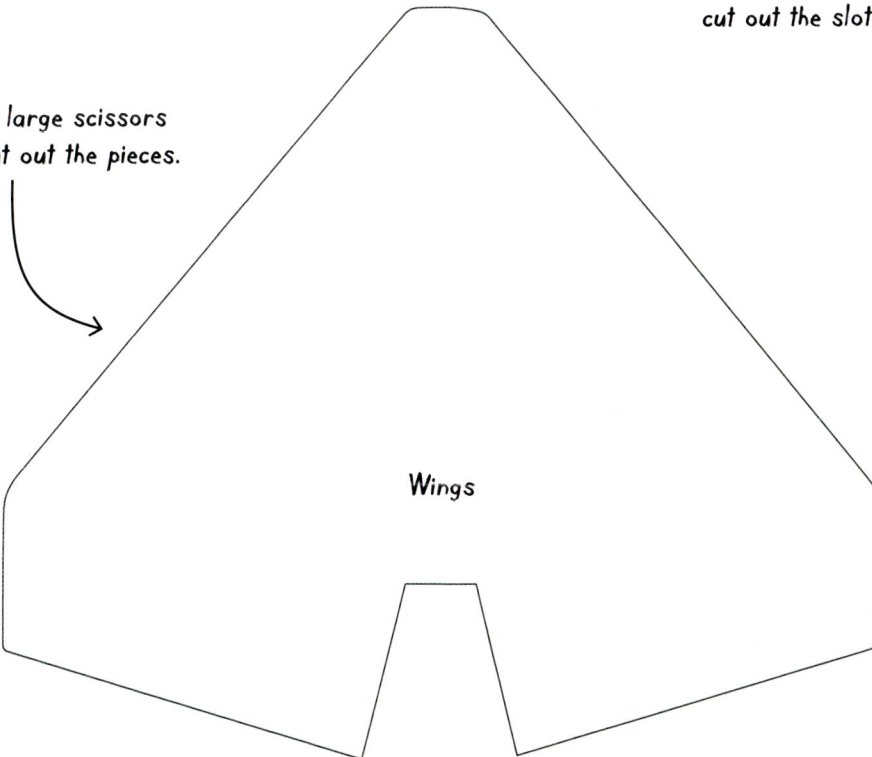

Wings

2 Place the template parts on the foam discs and draw around them.

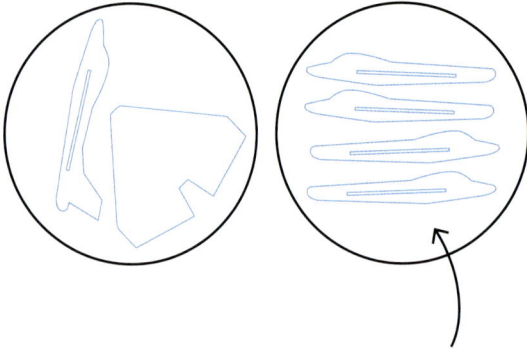

Draw around the outer body template twice one way up, then flip it over and draw around it twice the other way up.

3 Cut out the parts with large scissors and the slots with nail scissors. Make sure that each slot is big enough for the wing section to slide through.

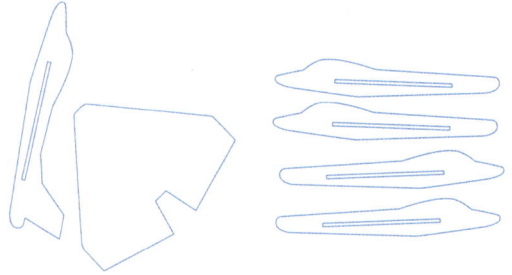

⚠ *Alternatively, ask an adult to cut out the parts using a craft knife.*

4 Sandwich the body parts together, as shown, then check that the slot in the wings is wide enough for the body to fit into.

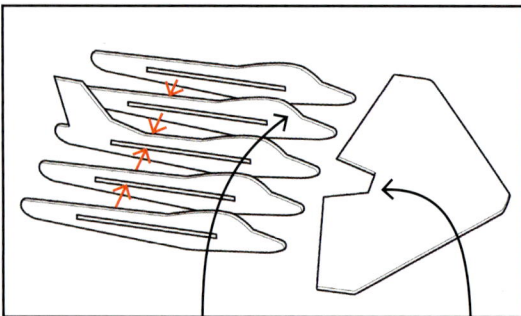

Make sure any dimpled sides face the middle.

The body needs to fit here. Widen the gap if necessary.

5 Slide the body over one wing until the back of the body fits into the wing slot, as shown. Then slide the front of the body over the front of the wings.

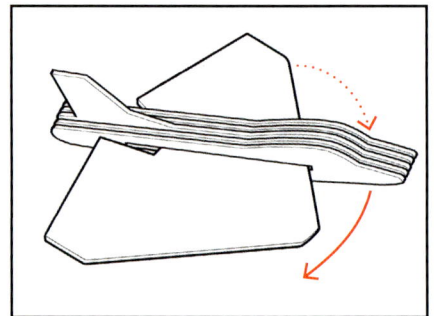

Adjust the body position to make the glider as symmetrical as possible.

16

6 Bend a large paper clip to fit closely over the nose. Tape the back of the body parts together.

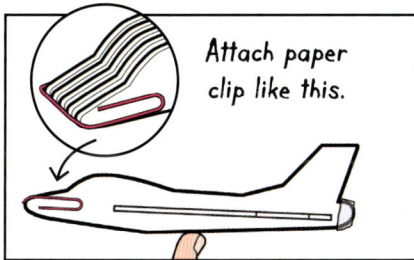

Attach paper clip like this.

Balance the glider on your finger—it should balance about halfway along.

7 Launch your glider as shown, and watch how it flies!

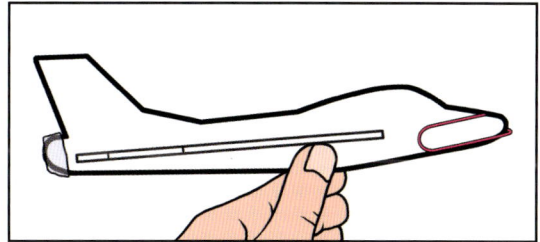

Hold and throw!

NOW YOU CAN...

★ Make improvements! Try to stop the nose from tilting up or down too much by adjusting the size or number of paper clips.

★ Try bending the wings up slightly as shown to make a very shallow V shape—this can help the glider to fly straight.

★ Try bending the back of the wings up very slightly to make the nose of the glider tilt up when in flight. But don't bend too much or the glider will try to climb, slow down, and stop flying, or "stall."

HOW IT WORKS

Gliders are aircraft without engines. They are relatively lightweight and have large wings that help them to stay up in the air. As the glider travels forward (and slightly downward) through the air, the smooth flow of air under and over the wings creates an upward lift that opposes the downward pull of gravity.

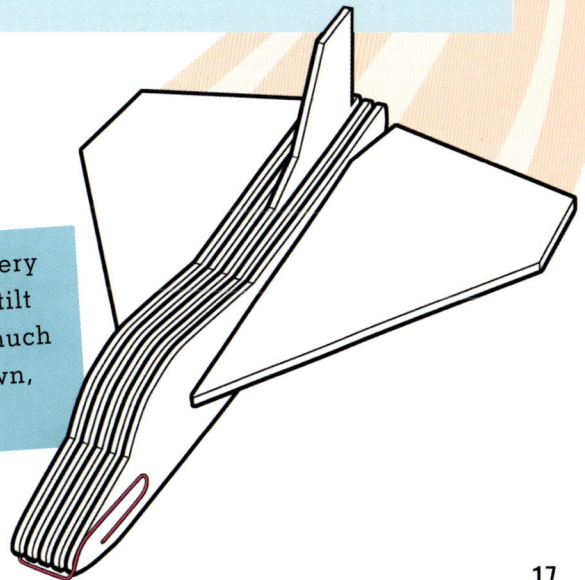

17

STOMP ROCKET

Make a mobile rocket launcher to send an air-powered rocket high into the sky.

⚠ **TAKE CARE** using nail scissors—ask an adult to start the cut. Don't fire the rocket near people.

1 Wrap double-sided foam tape around one end of the hose and push it into the soda bottle —it must fit tightly in the neck. Secure with duct tape.

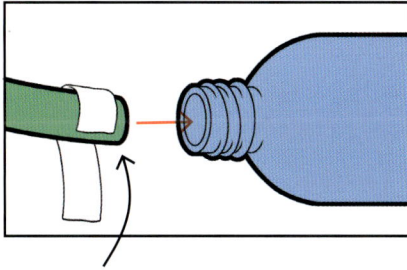

Remove the plastic backing from the foam tape as you wind it so the tape sticks together properly.

2 ⚠️ Put the marbles or pebbles into the milk jug to stop it from falling over. Make a hole just below the handle. Push the hose into the hole and out of the jug's neck.

Use nail scissors to make the hole—ask an adult to help you.

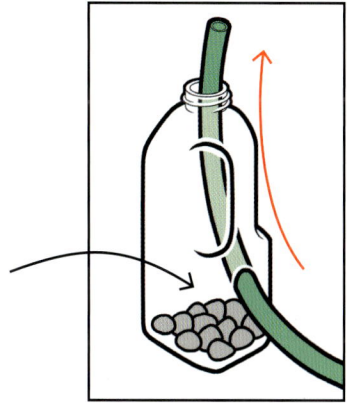

3 ⚠️ Clamp the tube gently in the vise and saw off 8 inches. Smooth off the end. Cut a hole in the milk jug cap the same size as the end of the tube.

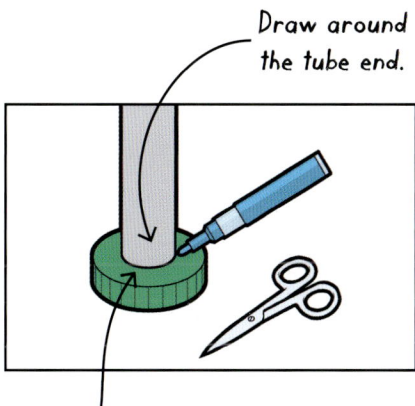

Draw around the tube end.

Cut out the circle with nail scissors. (In step 7 you'll fit the tube into the hole and it will need to be a tight fit.)

4 To make the cardstock rocket, cut out a 6-inch square of cardstock and roll it around the tube. Put tape around it, as shown, then stick tape all the way along the seam.

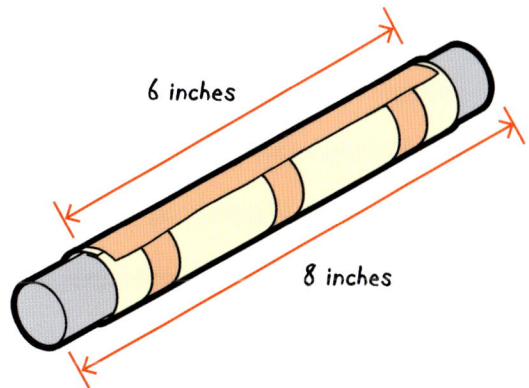

6 inches

8 inches

The cardstock must be closely wrapped around the tube, but loose enough to slide easily along it.

5 Cut out a cardstock disc and tape it to the end of the rocket. Blow through the tube to check that your rocket flies off the tube easily.

Tape on the cardstock disc.

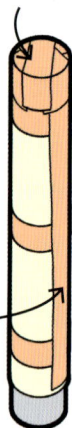

Make sure all the seams are airtight.

Blow through this end.

6 Wrap double-sided foam tape around the end of the hose that's sticking out of the top of the milk jug and push it into the tube. Secure with duct tape.

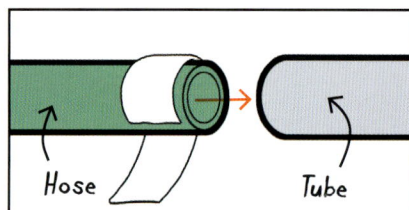

Hose

Tube

Remove the plastic backing from the foam tape as you wind it.

Make sure the seal is airtight.

7 Slide the milk jug cap down the tube until it touches the top of the duct tape, then screw it onto the milk jug. Slide the rocket onto the tube.

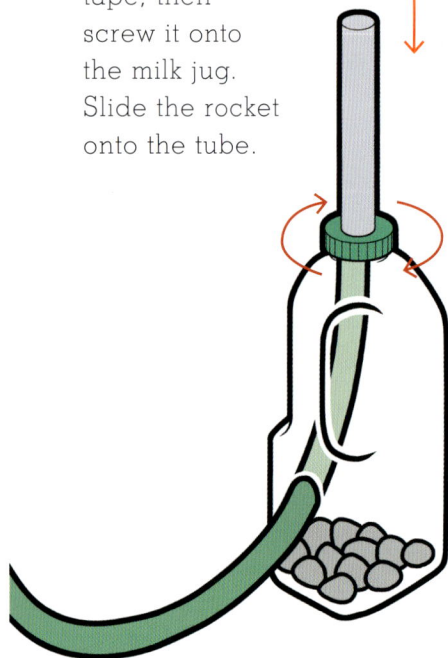

8 Stomp hard on the soda bottle to fire the rocket. Blow down the tube to recharge the soda bottle with air for your next rocket launch.

⚠️ Don't fire the rocket near people.

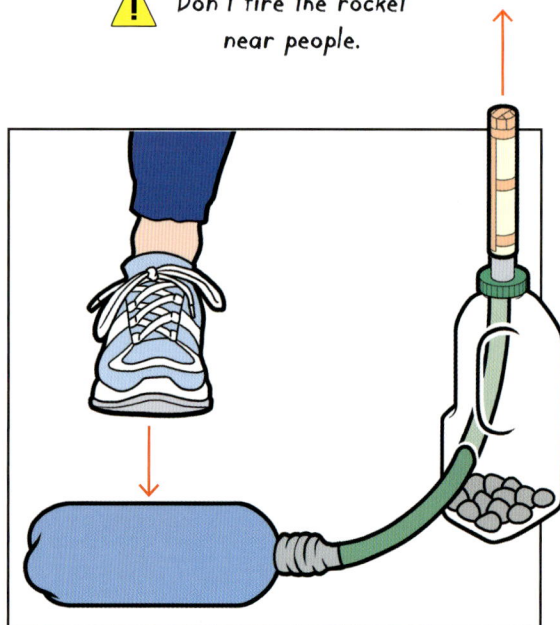

HOW IT WORKS

When you stomp on the soda bottle, you force air along the hose and up the tube into the rocket. This pushes the rocket off the end of the tube, allowing the air to escape. If the rocket fits too tightly on the tube, then the friction between them will make it difficult for the rocket to launch. If it is too loose, then air can escape easily down the sides so the rocket won't go as high.

NOW YOU CAN...

* Make a nose cone for your rocket from a semicircle of cardstock. Tape up the seam and attach it to your rocket. The cone should help the rocket to fly straight and make it more streamlined, so it cuts through the air more easily.

* Make some cardstock fins for your rocket, about 2 ½ inches long. The fins help to keep the rocket pointing in the direction of travel instead of tumbling through the air.

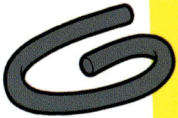

* Try to get your rocket to go higher by using a larger diameter hose, such as a bicycle inner tube. Using a shorter, wider tube should make it easier for the air to pass through.

* Try making rockets out of thinner or thicker cardstock to see which goes higher.

Square section wood
1/2 inch x 1/2 inch x 3 feet long

2 countersunk Pozidriv®
screws, size 6 x 5/8"

5 plastic bottle caps

2 pieces of wooden skewer
4 1/2 inches long

2 pieces of 1/4-inch-diameter
rod x 3 1/2 inches long

1 toothpick

4 countersunk Pozidriv®
screws size 6 x 1"

2 rubber bands—one roughly
1/16 inch x 1/8 inch x 6 inches
long; one 1/16 inch x 1/8 inch x
3 inches long

Pompom or similar
lightweight missile

FROM YOUR TOOLBOX:

• ruler • pencil • junior
hacksaw • vise • sandpaper
• bradawl • drill with drill
bits 5/64", 3/32", 9/64", 1/4",
5/16" (a pillar drill would be
even better) • Pozidriv®
screwdriver • double-sided
foam tape • large scissors
• masking tape • pencil
sharpener • adhesive
putty • hammer • small
pruning shears

CATAPULT

Create your very own ancient siege
weapon to bombard the enemy ramparts!

TAKE CARE using the saw and drill—ask an adult for help. Take care with the sharp pencil.
Only adults should use the small pruning shears. Only fire lightweight missiles.

1 Look at the picture and try to figure out what each part of the catapult does. Which parts move and which parts stay still?

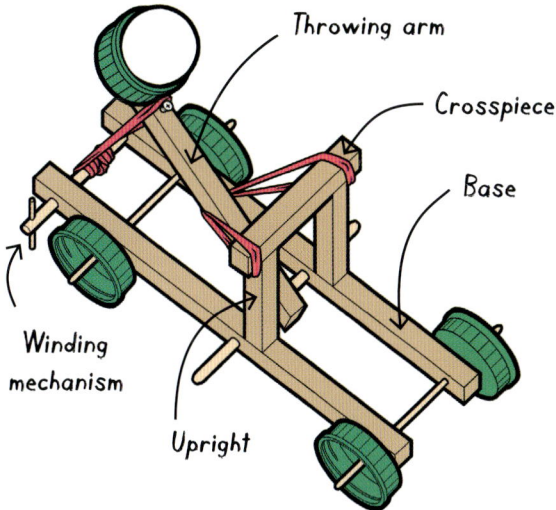

Throwing arm

Crosspiece

Base

Winding mechanism

Upright

THROWING ARM

2 ⚠ To make the throwing arm, saw off 6 3/4 inches of wood. Smooth all the edges with sandpaper. Make two marks, as shown.

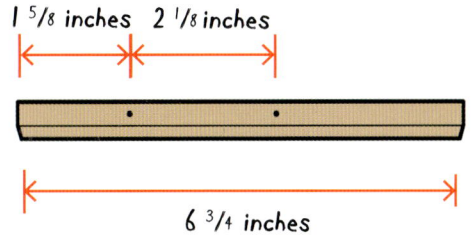

1 5/8 inches   2 1/8 inches

6 3/4 inches

To avoid splitting the wood when sawing it, turn it over just before you break through and cut from the other side.

3 ⚠ Indent the two marks, then drill 3/32"-diameter holes all the way through. Smooth with sandpaper. Screw in the size 6 x 5/8" screws, one from the top and one from the bottom, leaving the heads sticking out 3/16 inch.

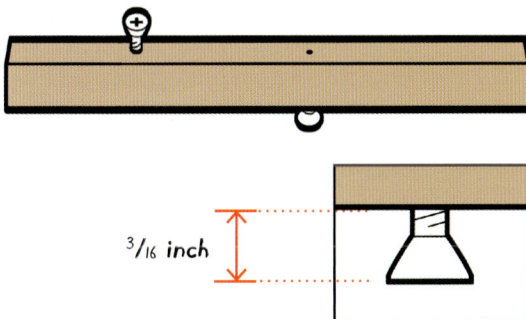

3/16 inch

Be careful to hold the drill straight or you may snap the drill bit.

4 Attach a bottle cap to the top using double-sided tape—make sure you leave a gap between the cap and the screw head for the rubber band. Mark a hole position in the side, as shown.

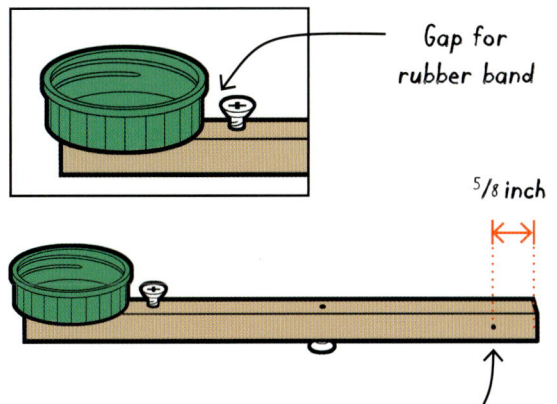

Gap for rubber band

5/8 inch

Make sure the mark for the hole is on the center-line of the wood.

5 ⚠️ Clamp the wood firmly in the vise to stop it from splitting, make an indent on the mark, drill a $^3/_{32}$" pilot hole, then enlarge it to $^5/_{16}$". Smooth the wood with sandpaper.

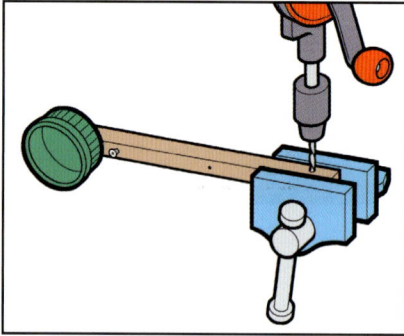

Making an indent helps you to drill in the right place.

BASE

6 ⚠️ For the base, cut two 10 $^1/_4$-inch lengths of wood. Tape them together with masking tape. Mark, indent, and drill four $^9/_{64}$" holes, as shown, through both pieces of wood.

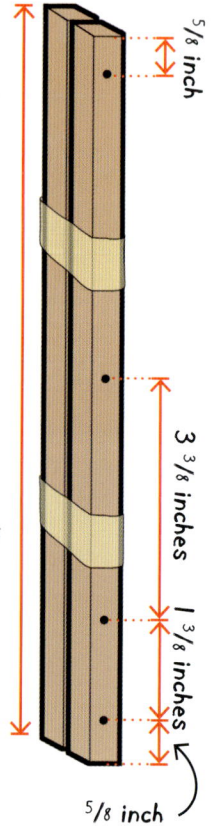

10 $^1/_4$ inches

$^5/_8$ inch

3 $^3/_8$ inches

1 $^3/_8$ inches

$^5/_8$ inch

The holes need to stay on the center line through both pieces of wood, so hold the drill very straight.

7 ⚠️ Mark, indent, and drill a $^9/_{64}$" hole in the top of each base piece. (These holes will be used to attach the crosspiece at step 20.) Remove the masking tape.

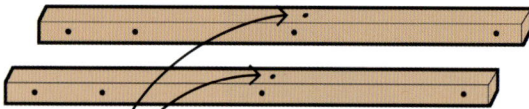

These holes are at right angles to the other holes.

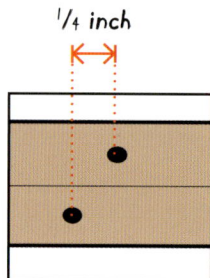

$^1/_4$ inch

8 ⚠️ Clamp each piece and enlarge the central hole in the side to $^1/_4$" and the end hole shown to $^5/_{16}$". Smooth with sandpaper.

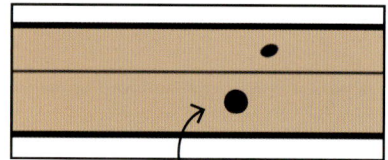

Enlarge the central side holes to $^1/_4$".

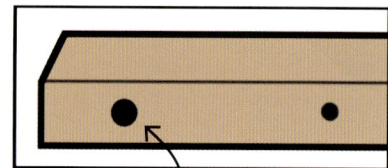

Enlarge the holes at this end to $^5/_{16}$".

9 Slightly sharpen the rod and skewer ends. Clamp one part of the base and fit a rod into the central $1/4$" hole and the skewers into the $9/64$" holes.

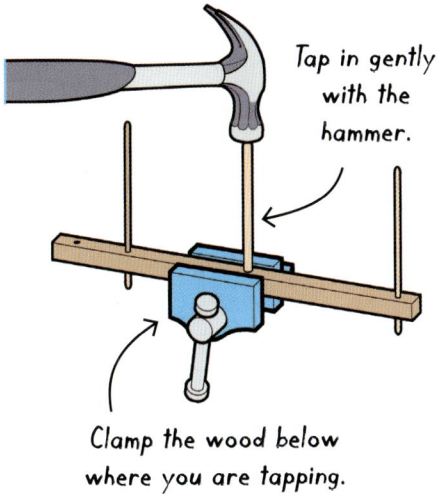

Tap in gently with the hammer.

Clamp the wood below where you are tapping.

10 Slide the throwing arm onto the rod. Push the second side of the base onto the skewers and rod, leaving a gap of $1 \ 1/2$" between the base parts.

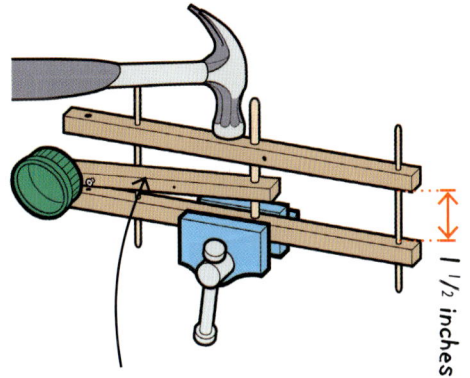

$1 \ 1/2$ inches

Make sure you fit the throwing arm the right way around.

WHEELS

11 ⚠ Push each of the remaining bottle caps, open end downward, onto a lump of adhesive putty. Use a sharp pencil to make a hole in the middle of each one, then push the caps, open ends facing out, onto the skewers.

Keep the pencil upright or the lead may snap.

Ask an adult to trim off the ends of the skewers with small pruning shears.

The hole needs to be a tight fit on the skewer.

The wheels are not intended to rotate.

WINDING MECHANISM

12 ⚠ To make the winding mechanism, clamp the remaining rod in the vise. Mark, indent, and drill a $5/64$" hole right through, $1/4$ inch from the end.

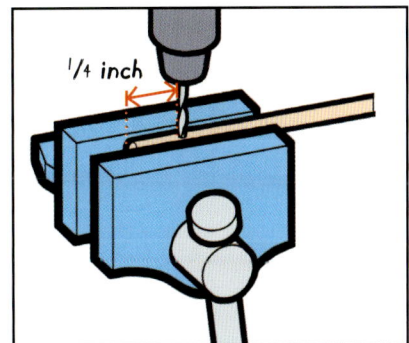

$1/4$ inch

Be careful to hold the drill straight or you may snap the drill bit.

13 ⚠️ Mark, indent, and drill another $5/64"$ hole at the other end, but make this hole roughly at right angles to the first hole, as shown. Smooth with sandpaper.

1/4 inch

The two holes should be roughly at right angles.

14 ⚠️ Slide the rod into the $9/32"$ holes in the base and make sure it rotates easily.

If the rod doesn't turn easily, run the $9/32"$ drill through the holes again.

UPRIGHTS

15 Use the scissors to snip the tips off a toothpick, then cut it in half. Tap the pieces gently into the $5/64"$ holes so they stick out an equal length on both sides.

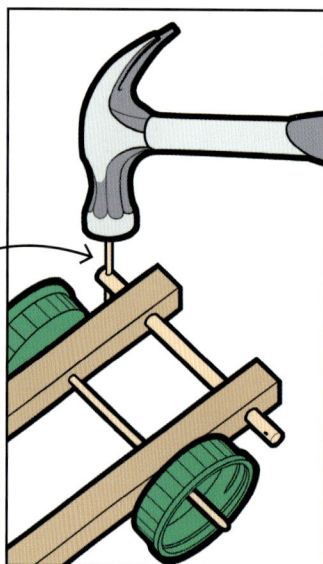

If the toothpicks touch the bottle caps, trim them slightly shorter.

16 Wrap a piece of masking tape around the $3/32"$ drill bit, $5/8$ inch from its tip. This will help you to drill the right depth hole in the uprights (see step 17).

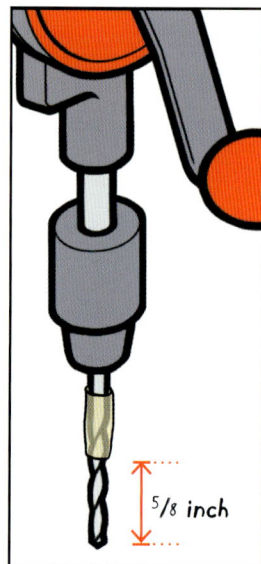

When the masking tape touches the wood, you'll know your hole is the right depth.

$5/8$ inch

17 For the uprights, cut and sand two 1 $3/4$-inch lengths of square section wood. Clamp as shown, then indent and drill a $3/32$"-diameter hole at each end, $5/8$ inch deep.

Hold the drill straight and drill in the middle of the wood.

CROSSPIECE

18 To make the crosspiece, cut a 3 $1/8$-inch length of square section wood and mark, indent, and drill two $9/64$"-diameter holes, as shown.

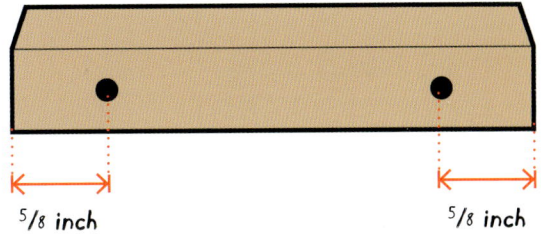

$5/8$ inch $5/8$ inch

Smooth all sides and edges so that they won't damage the rubber band.

19 Tightly screw two 1-inch-long screws through the holes in the crosspiece and into the holes in the uprights, as shown. Remove from the vise.

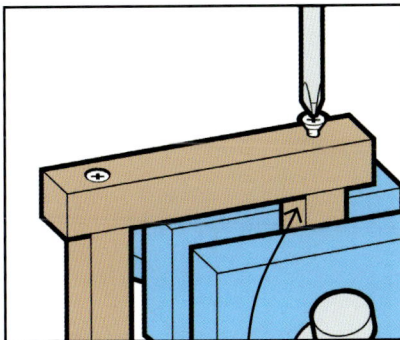

Clamp each upright in the vise before you screw into it.

20 Clamp the crosspiece upside down. Holding the throwing arm against the winding mechanism, screw the base tightly to the crosspiece uprights, as shown, using the holes drilled at step 7.

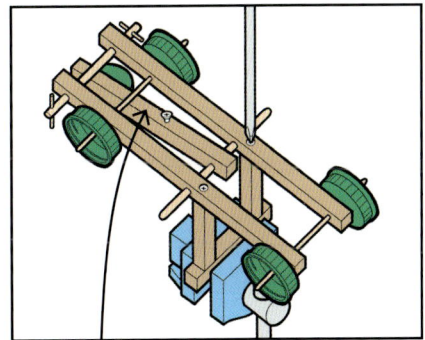

Make sure the throwing arm is at the winding mechanism end.

FIRING MECHANISM

21 Pass the 3-inch-long rubber band under the throwing arm and hook it over the ends of the crosspiece, as shown.

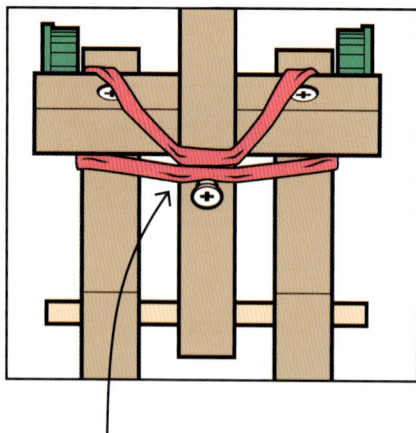

The rubber band should sit just above the screw head.

22 Loop the 6-inch-long rubber band (or two shorter rubber bands looped together) around the winding mechanism.

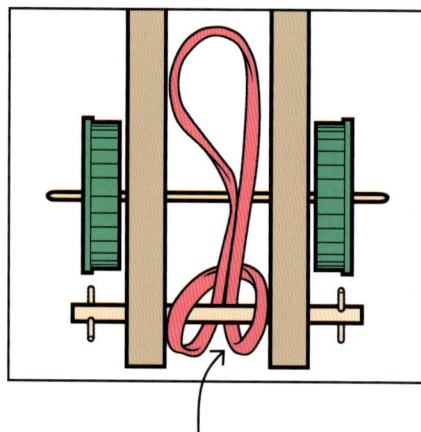

Loop it this way around. If you loop it the other way, it slips.

23 Pull the rubber band tight around the rod so it doesn't slip when winding up. Hook it over the throwing arm between the bottle cap and screw head.

Hook the rubber band just above the screw head.

24 ⚠️ Wind the arm back to prime your catapult and place a missile in the cap, as shown. To fire, let go of the winding mechanism abruptly.

Take aim and FIRE!

Wind here by turning the toothpicks.

HOW IT WORKS

When you wind back the throwing arm, elastic potential energy is stored in the stretched rubber band, which will pull the arm forwards. When you let go, much of this energy is converted to kinetic (movement) energy of the arm and the missile, while some is converted to heat and sound. The throwing arm and missile move together until the arm hits the crosspiece and stops, while the missile continues.

NOW YOU CAN...

Ping pong ball

* Try catapulting different lightweight missiles to see which goes farthest.

* Fit different rubber bands to try to improve performance.

* Try holding the base still as you fire to stop the catapult moving—see if this makes the missile go farther.

* Raise the front of the base up, for example on a book, to see what effect it has.

* Try using a deeper bottle lid on the throwing arm.

* Invite your friends around to make catapults and hold a competition to see who can fire the farthest.

GLOSSARY

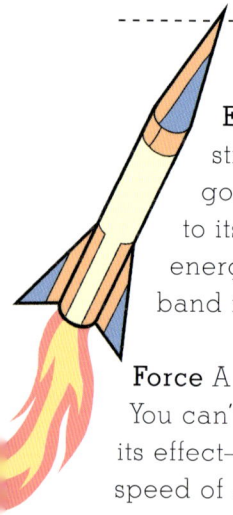

Elastic potential energy If you stretch a rubber band and then let go, the rubber band should return to its original shape. The type of energy stored in the stretched rubber band is called elastic potential energy.

Force A force can be a push or a pull. You can't see it, but you can often see its effect—a force can change the speed of an object, its direction of movement, or its shape.

Friction A force between surfaces that are sliding, or trying to slide, across each other. Friction is often useful—for example, it stops bicycle tires from slipping on the road.

Gravity A force that pulls things down and makes things fall to the ground. The more mass an object has, the more force will be pulling it down.

Kinetic (movement) energy The energy an object has because it is moving. The faster an object moves, and the more mass it has, the more kinetic energy it will have.

Lift The force that pushes an airplane upward to keep it in the air, opposing gravity, which is pulling it down toward the ground.

Streamlined A streamlined object has a shape designed to reduce resistance to movement through water or air, so that the object can pass through more easily and quickly.

Symmetrical A symmetrical shape is the same on both sides of a central dividing line.

Template A shaped piece of material used as a pattern for drawing or cutting around.

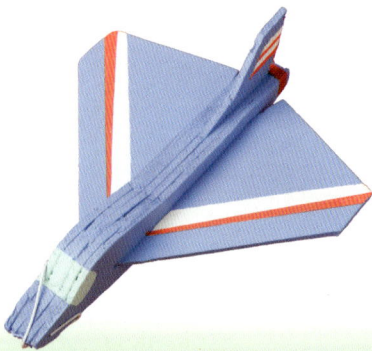

FIND OUT MORE

For more STEM ideas and activities check out these websites:

www.exploratorium.edu/explore
www.howtosmile.org
www.lawrencehallofscience.org

LOOK OUT FOR THESE

You can find lots more exciting STEM projects for budding engineers here:

MOVE IT!
7 creative STEM projects for budding ENGINEERS

CAROLINE ALLISTON

Projects
Cartesian Diver
Sailboat
Balloon Buggy
Marble Run
Coloured Spinner
Marble Maze
Orbiting in Space

WIRE IT!
6 creative STEM projects for budding ENGINEERS

CAROLINE ALLISTON

Projects
Coin Battery
Handheld Fan
Flashlight
Steady Hand Game
Fan Boat
Vibrating Brush Monster

CODE IT!
4 creative STEM projects for budding ENGINEERS

CAROLINE ALLISTON

Projects
Lighthouse
Traffic Lights
Chair-o-plane
Motorized Car

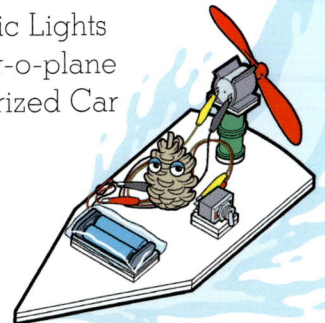

INDEX

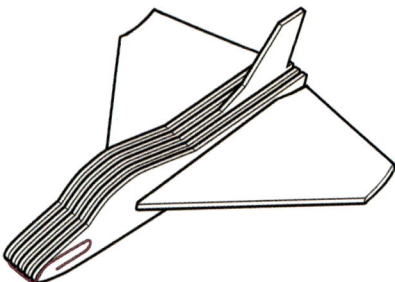